CABBAGETOWN

THE STORY OF A VICTORIAN NEIGHBOURHOOD

PENINA COOPERSMITH

PHOTOGRAPHY BY VINCENZO PIETROPAOLO

FOREWORD BY GEORGE H. RUST-D'EYE

JAMES LORIMER AND COMPANY, PUBLISHERS
TORONTO, 1998

James Lorimer & Company Ltd. acknowledges the support of the Department of Canadian Heritage and the
Ontario Arts Council in the development of writing and
publishing in Canada. We acknowledge the support of the
Canada Council for the Arts for our publishing program.

Cover design: Kevin O'Reilly
Cover photo: Vincenzo Pietropaolo

Canadian Cataloguing in Publication Data

Coopersmith, Penina
  Cabbagetown: the story of a Victorian neighbourhood

ISBN 1-55028-579-3

1. Cabbagetown (Toronto, Ont.) — History.
2. Cabbagetown (Toronto, Ont.) — Tours. 3. Toronto
(Ont.) — History. 4. Toronto (Ont.) — Tours. I. Title.
FC3097.52.C66 1997   971.3'541   C97-931877-7
F1059.5.T686C32 1997

James Lorimer & Company Ltd., Publishers
35 Britain Street
Toronto, Ontario
M5A 1R7

Printed and bound in Canada

Credits and Acknowledgments

I want to thank the many Cabbagetowners from whose knowledge and love of their community I benefitted in preparing this book, especially Rollo Meyer, George Rust-D'Eye, and Constance Madelina. And, also, my daughter Aviva who patiently trod the streets of Cabbagetown with me.

Photo Credits

Legend: T = Top; B = Bottom; L = Left; R= Right
The following images appear courtesy of:

City of Toronto Archives: 9T (9.2.3.6. No. 795); 15T (James Collection, SC244-50.1); 42T; 43B (SC 246-20N); 46T; 49T (James Collection, SC244-7.27); 52 (SC246 No.2-N); 53B; 55B; (Health Dept. No. 339); 58T (James Collection, 100224); 58B; 59 (James Collection, SC244-8.3); 61 (Housing Dept. No. 9); 63 (9.2.3.W Misc. No. 798); 64T (Globe and Mail Collection,1324310; 65B (Globe and Mail Collection, 1322434)

Heritage Toronto: 23

Jefferys, C.W., Estate Archive: 21 (C.W. Jefferys [1869-1951], *Lieut. Governor Simcoe Building Fort York*, 1794, n.d. [c. 1934], oil on board [46.7 x 50.0 cm [sight]); collection of F.K. Venables, Ottawa. Photo: T.E. Moore Photography Inc., Toronto. Reproduced with permission of C.W. Jefferys Estate Archive, Toronto.

Metropolitan Toronto Reference Library: 10 (T11459); 15BL (T13251); 18T (T11506); 18B; (T11505); 20 (T18042); 22 (789 U2); 24 (T10722); 25 (T12031); 28T (T 31473); 29B; 31 (T10914); 38T (T10970); 38B (T11454); 39 (T11774); 40B (T13045); 43T (T33502); 44B (968-12-658); 45 (968-12-566); 50T (T30536); 54 (984-3-135D); 56L (T11761); 56R; 57

Royal Ontario Museum: 16T (*View of the Simcoe Property in Upper Canada*, 954.100.5 © ROM)

Rust-D'Eye, George: 32T; 35; 40T; 41; 78B; 88; 98BR

Task Force to Bring Back the Don: 49B

Vachon, Alexa: 3B (location courtesy of Quattrocentro Design)

All other photographs were taken by Vincenzo Pietropaolo.

CONTENTS

FOREWORD

Penina Coopersmith's short book reflects a continuing interest in Cabbagetown expressed both locally and abroad.

Recently, when the Congress for the New Urbanism held their annual conference in Toronto, they requested a walking tour of Cabbagetown and Regent Park. A few years ago, when the American Planning Association and the Ontario Professional Planners Institute held a joint conference in Toronto, they, too, arranged for a tour of Cabbagetown.

Tours led by the Cabbagetown Preservation Association are always well attended, and the Association is frequently called upon to conduct excursions for various organizations. At any given time, there are almost as many walking tours on the streets of Cabbagetown as there are film crews!

Why the interest in Cabbagetown?

As suggested in this book, the bulk of what is today considered Cabbagetown occupies not much more than a square kilometre of fairly densely packed small houses. The area contains no architectural masterpieces, nor is there a record of any event of great historical significance ever happening there. Historically, the area played no major role in the planning and development of the City of Toronto.

What, then, has driven the obvious widespread interest in the neighbourhood? What led people like Hugh Garner, J. Vernon McAree, Bill Hambly, me, and now Penina Coopersmith to write about the character and history of Cabbagetown?

Cabbagetown is important. It is important for its physical form, for its colour and traditions, and for its contribution to Toronto as "the city that works."

Although, as outlined in the book, the boundaries of Cabbagetown have never been precise, have never been recognized officially, and have never remained static for any length of time, there have been, and are, areas between Sherbourne Street and the Don River south of Bloor Street typified by narrow streets lined with Victorian houses, which represent the physical embodiment of what people call "Cabbagetown."

Carlton St.

Today's Cabbagetown, represented by that part of the previously described area north of Gerrard Street East, includes virtually unbroken streetscapes of homes built before the turn-of-the-century, most of them before 1890. Few of the houses were designed by architects, and few were built for wealthy or even upper-middle-class residents, but all of them, in their scale, texture, colour, and incredible diversity of architectural devices and decoration, come together to form a unique, interconnected whole.

Parliament St.

Penina Coopersmith describes how and why these results were produced and outlines the stages of the area's development. She also touches on the non-residential developments in the area — the early industries at its periphery, the Toronto General Hospital, the schools and churches, and, particularly, the importance of its two significant cemeteries.

The book traces the origins of Cabbagetown back to the area around Parliament, south of Queen, just east of the original Town of York established in 1793. From its settlement in the 1840s and 1850s, Penina Coopersmith looks at Cabbagetown's physical and social development. The themes discussed in the book provide an explanation for the amazing perseverence of the neighbourhood. The

Entrance to Riverdale Farm

story is brought up-to-date with the political changes in Toronto since the 1970s, by addressing the role played by David Crombie, John Sewell, and Karl Jaffary in preserving present-day Cabbagetown through a period of rapid change.

Today Toronto is known internationally as a safe, clean city that has avoided many of the problems that beset other North American cities. There is no doubt it has a deservedly envied reputation as an attractive city in which to live and do business, a reputation barely yet exploited in terms of tourism and economic development. Those of us who have witnessed the changes in Toronto over the past quarter of a century are well aware of the immense satisfaction derived from living in an historic community so close to the amenities of the central city.

Penina Coopersmith manages to pack an amazing number of facts based, obviously, on considerable research, into a short, easy-to-read, and welcome book. This is the type of book to enjoy in one sitting, preferably while relaxing on a bench in Riverdale Park or Allan Gardens on a warm spring day — the best time to tour Cabbagetown, before the greening of our ubiquitous trees, bushes, and ivy.

There is no doubt that a reader's visit to this book, like a visit to Cabbagetown itself, will be well rewarded.

— George H. Rust-D'Eye

Winchester St.

INTRODUCTION

Consider the cabbage. It is an ordinary vegetable, admittedly full of vitamins, but nonetheless, probably not a food one would cross the street to sample, let alone travel a great distance to obtain. Yet it was once regarded as a delicacy and held in high esteem.

The opposite is true of Cabbagetown. Originally a pejorative term for a down-at-the-heels neighbourhood inhabited by British working-class residents who grew and boiled this globular gaseous green, Cabbagetown has become a synonym for a vibrant, quirky, "with-it" community. It is home to a complex mixture of social groups that share in common an enormous pride in their neighbourhood. Today, the cabbage is resplendent on flags and signposts or grown in front yards as an ornamental plant.

Cabbagetown draws urbanists, architects, planners, and historians as well as visitors from around the globe. They come to see one of North America's largest collections of late nineteenth-century homes, and the miracle of a neighbourhood that works in a city that works. This book provides visitors and residents alike with a brief overview of Cabbagetown's trans-

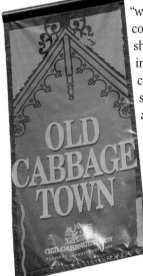

Cabbagetown banner

formation from a primeval forest, to what was described as "North America's only Anglo-Saxon slum," to a thriving community set amidst increasingly re-greened surroundings. The intention here is not to give a detailed account of the history of the area, but to provide a sense of what Cabbagetown has looked like and felt like to those who experienced each of its many guises.

Given Cabbagetown's inordinately strong sense of identity, it is particularly peculiar that no one agrees on its location. Only its eastern boundary — the Don River — provokes no dispute. Its southern, northern, and western edges are a matter of contention. The Cabbagetown Business Improvement Association, and

143 Amelia St.

those who prepare walking tours for Toronto, draw its boundaries most narrowly, including only the area bounded by Gerrard Street, Parliament Street, the northern edge of St. James Cemetery and the Don River.

There is no denying that this is the most picturesque part of the community. But old-timers, especially the more curmudgeonly among them, will dispute that this area is Cabbagetown at all. For them, the real Cabbagetown no longer exists. It was located to the south of the one we know today, and it disappeared when its homes and stores were demolished in the 1950s and 1960s to make way for

Parliament St., 1949

Regent Park, a public housing development.

If you take the view, however, that a community — no matter how diverse its components — is defined over time by its shared experience, then a more liberal definition of the place will seem appropriate. In the eighteenth century, Lieutenant Governor John Graves Simcoe set aside for government use a 40-hectare "Park Lot" bounded by Queen Street on the south, Castle Frank on the the north, the Don River on the east and Berkeley Street on the west. Because settlement in Toronto moved north and west from the original townsite, rather than east, and because the Don River area was considered swampy and unhealthy, little of this particular Park Lot was

Alpha Ave. cottages

inhabited until well after Toronto's incorporation as a city in 1834.

In due course, industries set up shop in the east end, along Parliament Street, River Street or, like the distiller Gooderham and Worts, right on the lakefront, and workers encamped nearby. The area around King and Parliament Streets was the first, to see residential development, and from the beginning, it was a working-class neighbourhood. As Toronto's industry and population expanded, similarly modest, sometimes shoddy, working-class housing was built to the north, from the Don River on the east to as far west as the great mansions of Sherbourne Street. Throughout this area, the residents, although often quite poor, were almost exclusively white, Anglo-Saxon Protestants born in Canada or the British Isles. The few Catholics, mostly Irish, who settled in the area clustered in the blocks near King and Power Streets, an area that acquired the moniker "Corktown."

Starting in the 1850s, but especially after the 1870s, the district began to fill in. At least as far north as Gerrard Street, but in some blocks, all the way to St. James Cemetery, the houses were small, overcrowded, without plumbing, and often no better than shacks. There were exceptions, of course, primarily along Carlton and Winchester Streets, both of which were distinctively middle and upper middle class.

By the late 1930s, the entire area from the Don River almost to Yonge Street had become uniformly run down. The once-grand houses on Jarvis and Sherbourne Streets had become rooming houses, as had most of the bigger ones in Cabbagetown proper. It was in the wake of the demolition of the old Cabbagetown and the urban renewal of the 1960s, that today's Cabbagetown pulled itself together and carved out a new identity. Thus, the Cabbagetown we see on the eve of the twenty-first century is different from that of the nineteenth or even mid-twentieth century — different in character and, to some extent, in location.

For the purpose of this book, the Don River, Lake Ontario and St. James Cemetery will be taken as the east, south, and north boundaries of Cabbagetown. On the west, however, the boundary is harder to define. Parliament Street is often suggest-

John Ross Robertson's Sherbourne St. mansion, 1884

Carlton St.

Parliament St.

ed, but the area to the west of it was built up during the same period, has housed the same ethnic groups and experienced the same upheavals. So while the bulk of our discussion will focus on the area to the east of Parliament, occasional sorties will be made in a westerly direction.

The first chapter, "The Lay of the Land," examines the area's natural terrain, its geological underpinnings, its flora and fauna, and the ways in which two centuries of human settlement have affected the whole area, especially its most visible natural feature, the Don River. Also covered in this section are the earliest years of settlement in

Amelia St.

Riverdale Park

the region — virtually none of which was in Cabbagetown itself.

The second chapter, "Victorian Cabbagetown," covers the peak of residential and community growth which occurred in the 1840s and 1850s for the southern end of the area, and the 1870s through the 1890s for the remainder. It looks at the local and global events that created Cabbagetown and gave it its distinctive character. It also gives the reader a sense of what it was like to live, work, play, and pray in and around the community. Presented here as well are the major institutions built in

the area — the Toronto General Hospital, the Riverdale Zoo, and Allan Gardens.

For Cabbagetown, as for much of the rest of the world, the post-Victorian period has been a roller coaster. In the third chapter, "The Twentieth Century," we'll see what the darkest days of the two wars and the Depression did to the area and how World War II's aftermath of prosperity almost destroyed it. On the upswing, we'll see how the community rallied, what it has become — and is becoming. The book's concluding chapter presents two walking tours of the area.

1
LAY OF THE LAND

As with any place, many of the physical features that make Cabbagetown unique are the result of major geological events that occurred thousands to millions of years ago. And as with any place, even some of the more subtle historical features that make Cabbagetown unlike any other community — the fact that it was settled much later than most other parts of central Toronto, that it was largely working class — can also be attributed at least in part to geological or natural events that occurred in the distant past.

Take the distinctive brick, for instance, prevalent throughout Toronto, but ubiquitous in today's Cabbagetown. When the world was about four-hundred million years younger and fish were the earth's most advanced life form, a great shallow tropical sea

Red and white brick, Carlton St.

merged portions of Canada's Pre-Cambrian Shield. The stone that eventually defined a great triangular-shaped swath that runs from Collingwood to Metro Toronto is a gray shale interlaced with limestone. At its northern end, the Georgian Bay Formation, as it is called, is about 250 metres thick. In the Toronto area it is only 26 metres in depth.

covered much of southern Ontario. Over a period of about twenty-five million years, new layers of rock slowly were laid down at the bottom of this sea atop the sub-

This gray shale formation still would be widely visible today, instead of emerging in only a few outcroppings or after much excavation, had the past million years not

Don Brick Works, 1922

seen a series of four glaciers scrape their way back and forth over much of the continent, sculpting all that lay beneath them and relocating tons of material from one place to another. Among the materials left in Toronto by the last of these glaciers, the Wisconsinan, is a large clay deposit known as the Thorncliffe Formation. Stretching north and east from Queen's Park to the Don Valley, it is responsible for much of the brick we see in Cabbagetown today.

At one time, over a dozen brick works operated throughout this area, manufacturing the red brick common throughout Toronto, and the slightly less common "white" brick distinguished by what is really a creamy yellow hue.

Above Cabbagetown's slate and limestone foundation is a soil composition also unique to the area. Cabbages, like most vegetables, thrive in well-drained, slightly limey soil, and this is abundantly present throughout the area. Relatively recent alluvial deposits, primarily sandy in composition, were dumped by the Don River along its flood plain which, until a mere one hundred years ago, was far wider than might be assumed from looking at the River today. In fact, even at depths as great as 12 metres

Construction of the Bloor Viaduct, 1915

Don Valley, about 1790

The mouth of the Don River

below the floor of the Don Valley, the soil is predominantly sandy. Excavations in 1915 for the Bloor Street viaduct that connects Cabbagetown to the adjacent neighbourhood of Riverdale revealed strata of sand and silt containing logs, shells, nuts, and other riverine detritus.

Interspersed among the Don River's alluvial droppings are deposits of till — clay, gravel, and boulders — known as the Don Formation. Laid down during the Sagamonian period, the formation is evidence of a balmy break between glacial periods. Of greater influence on Cabbagetown's soil conditions than the Don Formation, however, were two early incarnations of Lake Ontario. The first, larger version was Lake Iroquois, formed at the time of the retreating ice, about eleven thousand years ago. From the Niagara River in the west to Trenton in the east, the edge of this body of water was 3 to 12 kilo-

Wildflowers near the Don River

metres farther north than today's Lake Ontario — except in Scarborough, where the old and new were congruent. This meant that today's Cabbagetown was partly submerged and that the mouth of the Don River was somewhere near O'Connor Drive. Over the thousands of years of Iroquois's existence, huge sandbars were deposited at the Don's mouth. When Lake Iroquois's level dropped some nine thousand years ago, the Don continued southward to find a new outlet. Not only did it carry some of that sand along with it on its new course, but below its former mouth it was deflected westward by all that sand. Thus it could be said that sand defines the eastern boundary of Cabbagetown.

Settlement

These geological and hydrological shifts were to influence the area's later settlement as well. Lake Fort Ann, the body of water that succeeded Lake Iroquois, actually was lower than today's Lake Ontario. As a result, the Don

Teasels growing in the Don Valley

Dr. Scadding showing the location of Castle Frank in the 1880s

River's new sand-accumulating mouth was south of its present location. When Lake Ontario rose to its current level, that mouth and much of the surrounding sand was covered by water. The Lake's currents shifted the sand and silt, creating the peninsula that later became the Toronto Islands and the immense swampy marshes and meadows that lay all around the mouth of the Don River when Europeans arrived. This marsh, felt to be hazardous to human health, contributed to the delay in the area's settlement until the mid-nineteenth century.

Another geographical feature that slowed Cabbagetown's development was the presence of Taddle Creek. The Creek flowed southeast from what is today the University of Toronto and across Queen's Park. It crossed Yonge Street between Shuter and Queen Streets, and then blocked off Queen (then called Lot) east of Church. From there it flowed south into the harbour

Castle Frank, the summer home of John Graves Simcoe, in the 1820s

near Ontario Street. Until the taming of the Taddle — mainly by burying it, sometimes by bridging it — its meandering hampered access to the areas north of Queen and east of Yonge.

About nine thousand years before the arrival of Europeans, however, various native groups — the stone-working Laurentian people, the pottery-making, tobacco-smoking Point Peninsula people, and ultimately, their descendants, the Iroquois people — began to visit the area. Apart from the remains of small encampments found along the Don River and a single, slightly more elaborate settlement near Riverdale Park, there is little to suggest that these early groups resided anywhere in Toronto for long periods. Their preference was for the more easily worked soils around Lake Simcoe and Georgian Bay, where they enjoyed fine fishing and hunting as well as access to the northern Algonquin peoples with whom they traded. Unlike the Humber and the Rouge Rivers, both of which permitted relatively easy portaging to Lake Superior via Georgian Bay, the Don River was never a major thoroughfare for these groups, the later fur traders, or even the early English settlers. Thus, when in the 1790s, the latter began to settle Toronto in earnest, the valley was in the state to which it had evolved naturally over nine thousand years.

It is difficult now, looking at Cabbagetown and the Don Valley, to imagine the area forested with huge stands of trees offering a perfect habitat for muskrats, rabbits, martens, Canada lynx, black bears, wolves, white-tailed deer, beaver, and the now-endangered cougar. Birdlife, too, was abundant, with enormous flocks of now-extinct passenger pigeons flying overhead, as well as terns, bitterns, gulls, and two species of eagles. Ospreys, wild turkeys, and grouse were also common. The large marshy area near the Don's mouth was said to be like a single thicket of wild willow and alder, with a variety of aquatic shrubbery, blue iris and bulrushes. Atlantic salmon were then to be found in Lake Ontario and and the Don was particularly noted for salmon fishing. As early as 1799, however, it was remarked that the salmon were being fished to extinction.

Although primeval, the area had a pastoral air, which may have been responsible for its appeal to Lady Simcoe,

Don River

Lieutenant Governor John Graves Simcoe's wife, who delighted in the Don Valley, sketched it and had their summer residence, Castle Frank, constructed overlooking the River where it meets what is now the Rosedale Ravine. Something of the Don Valley's early appeal — and the ways in which it differs from today — can be gleaned from C. Blackett Robinson's mid-nineteenth century description:

The Don winds through a broad valley, the bottom lands immediately adjoining the river, which are usually flooded in spring time, yielding rich pasturage. The

John Graves Simcoe, 1791, painted by Jean Laurent Mosnier

More dramatically, Toronto's first historian, Henry Scadding, whose father had been Simcoe's estate manager in England and had thereby acquired a large land grant, reminisced in the 1870s of a time when "springs gushed from the hillsides" and there were "dense forests of magnificent trees and a profusion of high shrubbery of wild willow, alder, whych-hazel, dogwood, and tree-cranberry … interwoven with the vine of the wild grape."

Whatever the attraction for Lady Simcoe, for her husband the Lieutenant Governor, the Don Valley's key charm was its thickly wooded banks, on which grew both deciduous trees — such as lime, basswood, sycamore, sassafras, various maple, oak, hickory, and elm — and tall conifers, mainly pine, an excellent resource for building what was to be a naval stronghold and government centre.

banks which are thickly wooded, rise abruptly, sometimes from the water, but more often at a considerable distance. They are broken by ravines, where tributary streams unite their waters with the Don, and occasionally these bluffs enclose a wide space giving an amphitheatre-like effect.

In 1794, Toronto was selected over Kingston and Newark (Niagara-on-the-Lake) as the capital and chief garrison of the newly created province of Upper Canada mainly because of its defensibility. The next step was ensuring that it was populated. Soldiers could, of course, be ordered to the garrison, and as a capital, no doubt some population

Lieut. Governor Simcoe Building Fort York, 1794, painted by C.W. Jefferys

Council-Office, Dec. 29, 1798.

YONGE-STREET.

NOTICE is hereby given to all perfons fettled, or about to fettle on *YONGE-STREET*, and whofe *locations* have not yet been confirmed by order of the PRESIDENT in council, that before fuch locations can be confirmed it will be expected that the following CONDITIONS be complied with :

First. That within *twelve months* from the time they are permitted to occupy their refpective lots, they do caufe to be erected thereon a good and fufficient dwelling houfe, of at leaft 16 feet by 20 in the clear, and do occupy the fame in *Perfon,* or by a fubftantial *Tenant.*

Second, THAT within the fame period of time, they do clear and fence *five* acres, of their refpective lots, in a fubftantial manner.

Third, THAT within the fame period of time, they do open as much of the Yonge-Street road as lies between the front of their lots and the middle of faid road, amounting to one acre or thereabouts.

JOHN SMALL, C. E. C.

Regulations for developing Yonge St., 1798

eventually would follow the officials who had no choice. But Simcoe seems to have wanted the place he called York to become a living, breathing town — a major commercial centre — rather quickly. At that point, however, most of the province's population of about 14,000 — many of whom had been Loyalists fleeing the United States, an influx not likely to repeat itself — lived near Kingston or Newark, and while neither community could boast York's natural harbour, both had other attractions and certainly were accessible by water. Somehow, people had to be attracted to a muddy backwater that might be subject to attack and, being largely sandy or clay-like, was not itself highly arable, although, as it turned out, the districts surrounding it varied from being good to excellent for farming.

Simcoe launched a thorough campaign to make his dream a reality. When he sailed across Lake Ontario from Newark and took up residence at York in 1793, he had Alexander Aitkin, a surveyor, draw up a simple town plan comprising ten perfectly square blocks in a two-row grid just north of Lake Ontario. For reasons that remain unfathomable, the townsite was east of the one proposed about a year earlier, quite some distance from Fort York and inhospitably close to the swampy meadows near the Don's mouth. To reinforce his belief that the Toronto Passage would prove commercially and strategically important, Simcoe had a road built from York northward 55 kilometres to Holland Landing from which Lake Simcoe and Georgian Bay could be accessed.

The road, called Yonge Street, was located several kilometres east of the

Fort York

old Humber Trail. Other roads were needed to render the capital more accessible to Newark and Kingston. To the west, the Dundas Road was constructed, running 120 kilometres to Newark; to the east, the Kingston Road, a 290-kilometre highway, was built. Their convergence at York made the town the hub of the province's surface transportation.

Thus the stage was set for future development. The icing on the cake, of course, was land. In addition to offering settlers townsites well outside the town at little or no cost, officials and other men of standing were eligible to receive one of the thirty-four "Park Lots" just adjacent to the town. These lots, 40.5 hectares each, ran north about 1.25 kilometres from a street one block above the townsite's northern boundary along Lot Street to the first concession, which became Bloor Street. It was not intended that this land be farmed, except perhaps in a gentlemanly sort of way, but it was obvious that were the town to prosper, these parcels of real estate would be immensely valuable. And indeed, the gentlemen to whom they went, and who actually settled on them, made up the well-heeled Family Compact that ran the city for more than a century.

The Cabbagetown Reserve

Two of the lots, however, did not go to gentlemen nor to anyone else. They were reserved for the Crown. Their fine timber was to be used for the construction of ships and, once depleted, they were to be the site of public buildings — the houses of parliament, the home of the lieutenant governor, a jail, perhaps a school. The bound-

York's first church, 1807

aries of these reserved lots were the Don River to the east, the first concession (Bloor Street) to the north, Berkeley Street to the west, and Lot Street (today's Queen Street) to the south, which, given the geography and location of the town, effectively meant to Lake Ontario. These, of course, were to become Cabbagetown's boundaries, and it was because the area

was set aside for these purposes — in addition to concerns about swamps and the like — that it was not settled, even as York gradually grew further east, north and west.

Gradually is a fairly critical word here. Whatever Simcoe's dreams, York grew slowly at first. Despite the arrival of government officials — and the shopkeepers, hoteliers, smiths, millers, and others needed to serve them — the population had reached only 756 by 1812. Of these, some seventy people lived in the Don Valley, primarily on the east side of the river. Some were farmers, others were millers.

The original provincial legislative buildings were constructed, as Simcoe intended, near the foot of Parliament Street, but the mansion that was to have been his official residence was considered too extravagant an expenditure. The very modest structures, which had only just been completed, were torched by the Americans in the War of 1812, and although rebuilt and enlarged in 1819, they burned again in 1824. But by then it had become unlikely that the Cabbagetown reserve would ever serve the institutional purpose for which it was intended. In 1797 a new town site had been drawn up to be situated to the west of the original ten-block site. The space between the two sites was set aside for public purposes, and early in the nineteenth century, it was here, between Jarvis and Bay Streets, that the market, the town's first church, its first school, the post-1824 legislative buildings and, ultimately, the community's civic buildings were to be constructed.

Although one of the first inns in York, the Jordan Hotel, opened in 1801 on what is now King Street between Berkeley and Ontario Streets, as late as 1834, development on the eastern edge of the original townsite was still sparse and virtually nothing had been built north of it. East of Parliament Street to the Don River, on the Park reserve, there was almost nothing. A rough road followed the shoreline to the Gibraltar Point Lighthouse, crossing the mouth of the Don River via a modest bridge. Another road, this one more heavily traversed, crossed the Don River at about Queen Street and headed east toward the more populous areas along the Kingston Road near what was to become the Beaches. A left-hand turn immediately after the Don would take one north along the Don Mills Road, now Broadview Avenue.

Setting the Stage

This may all seem a less than modest starting point for what was to become the crowded community of Cabbagetown. But just as large geological events laid the foundation for the shape and form of the area, so too, during this fallow early period, was the stage gradu-

Artist's conception of the Parliament Buildings on Front St. E., in the 1800s

ally being set for the growth of the neighbourhood. As early as 1811, a survey of the area east of the townsite laid out a number of streets south of Lot, and by 1830 the whole south end of the reserved Park Lots had been given to the Toronto Hospital as an endowment and the area had been re-surveyed and divided into parcels. By 1832, James Worts and his brother-in-law and partner William Gooderham had opened a grist mill for business on the newly available land. The Gooderham and Worts mill was to become the first of a number of enterprises near or along the lower Don River that required industrial workers. In the absence of public transit, the labourers of that time had no choice but to live within walking distance of their place of employment, thereby providing the basis for the growth of the adjacent working-class neighbourhood.

The Industrial Revolution as well as other events influenced the growth of Toronto and Cabbagetown.

First, ill-fated as the War of 1812 was for the modest government buildings on Parliament Street and for the future of Toronto as a garrison, the War's conclusion ensured stable relations with the Americans, making settlement throughout the area a less fearful prospect. The construction of the Erie and Welland Canals played a twofold role in the future of the city.

First, they gave rise to trade on the Great Lakes, enabling Toronto, and later Chicago and Thunder Bay, to flourish and compete for trade with their seaboard counterparts. Second, Toronto cut its financial teeth on the Welland Canal, giving birth to its growth as a commercial centre. And so, by the time the Irish potato famine of the 1840s caused hundreds of thousands to flee, Toronto had achieved sufficient critical mass to be among the immigrants' chief destinations. Why so many settled in Cabbagetown, and more interestingly, what they made of it, is the subject of the next chapter.

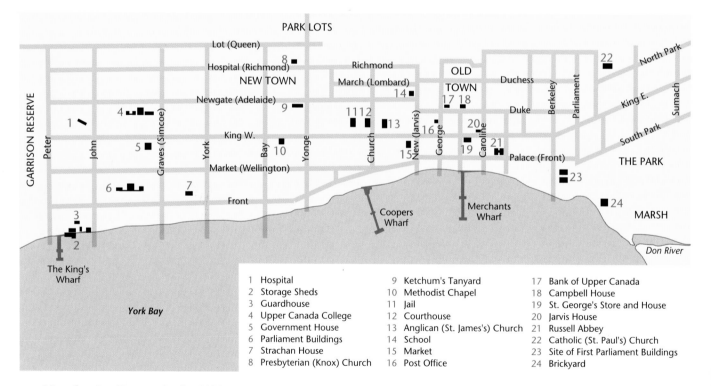

1 Hospital	9 Ketchum's Tanyard
2 Storage Sheds	10 Methodist Chapel
3 Guardhouse	11 Jail
4 Upper Canada College	12 Courthouse
5 Government House	13 Anglican (St. James's) Church
6 Parliament Buildings	14 School
7 Strachan House	15 Market
8 Presbyterian (Knox) Church	16 Post Office

17 Bank of Upper Canada
18 Campbell House
19 St. George's Store and House
20 Jarvis House
21 Russell Abbey
22 Catholic (St. Paul's) Church
23 Site of First Parliament Buildings
24 Brickyard

Map showing Toronto in the 1830s

The Stone Distillery, Gooderham and Worts, built about 1859

2
THE VICTORIAN ERA

Windmill on the Gooderham and Worts site, about 1834

In 1831 — six years before Queen Victoria ascended the throne — thirty-nine-year-old James Worts arrived in York from Suffolk, England, where he had owned a mill. He purchased some of the newly available land between Front Street and the lakeshore on the western side of the Don River. After rejecting the slow-moving lower Don as a power source, he began construction of a seventy-foot-high, red-brick windmill, which was completed and put into operation grinding flour in October 1832. By then, Worts's brother-in-law and partner, forty-two-year-old William Gooderham, also had arrived in York. It turned out, however, that the wind along the shore was not as steady as had been hoped, and the partners quick-

Gooderham and Worts

ly made arrangements to convert their mill to steam power. Some reports indicated that the windmill's sails were removed shortly after its use ceased, while others claim they blew off during great storms in the 1850s, but whatever the case, the unused windmill was for many years one of York's most notable landmarks.

A few years later, in 1834, the legislature of Upper Canada passed a bill entitled, "An Act to Extend the Limits of the Town of York, to Erect Said Town into a City, and to Incorporate It under the Name of the City of Toronto." The boundaries of the "newly-

Mill wheel

erected city" were Bathurst and Parliament Streets, Lake Ontario, and a line 366 metres north of Lot Street.

Beyond the city proper was an area called "the Liberties," which included what was to become Cabbagetown. Toronto's population at the time was 9,256, including those living in the Liberties, some 300 of whom are estimated to have lived in the Don Valley and the area between the Don and the eastern boundary of the original townsite.

In the same year, tragedy struck the Gooderham and Worts milling partnership when Worts's wife, who was Gooderham's sister, died in childbirth. Worts committed suicide soon after, leaving Gooderham to raise Worts's surviving children, in addition to his own brood of thirteen, and carry on the business. This Gooderham did to good advantage, recognizing by 1837 that some of the grain flowing in from newly settled regions of Upper Canada and — via the Welland Canal — the American mid-west could be distilled into liquor.

It is surprising that distilling did not become a major industry sooner. As early as April 1832 the editors of York's *Canadian Freeman*, a leading paper of the day, observed:

> It is really astonishing how the magistrates can allow the horrible nuisance which now appears on the face of this Bay. All the filth of the town — dead horses, dogs, cats, manure &c. heaped up together on the ice, to drop down, in a few days, into the water which is used by almost all the inhabitants on the Bay shore. If they have no regard for the health of their fellow-beings, are they not afraid to poison the fish that supply their own tables?

George Gooderham, son of founder William Gooderham

Clearly the town's water was not fit to drink. That very summer, in fact, cholera killed some 273 people. About double that number died during the summer of 1834. Other outbreaks occurred in 1849 and 1854, with 424 and 500 fatalities respectively. Germs, of course, had yet to be discovered, but even at the time of the first outbreak, it was widely accepted that filthy water and the "miasmas" of swamps, such as the huge one adjacent to the lower Don River, were unhealthy. Little wonder that early travellers to the Canadas remarked on the large number of taverns — at least spirits were safe to drink. Little wonder, too, that toward the end of the nineteenth century, when water had again been made potable, the temperance movement began to gain a major foothold in Toronto.

By the 1860s, brewing had become a major industry in Toronto. In addition to pioneers like Gooderham — and later his sons and Wort's nephews — there was Enoch Turner, who was a

Chester Springs Marsh and the Bloor Viaduct

We hope that His Excellency will take cognizance of the state of the Bay from the Garrison down, and see the carrion-broth to which the worshipful magistracy are about to treat the inhabitants when the ice dissolves. There is not a drop of good well-water about the Market-square, and the people are obliged to use the Bay water however rotten… There is nothing more conducive to health than good water — nothing more destructive than bad — and what ought the authorities to watch over and protect before the health of the community?

Todmorden Mills

Toronto Rolling Mills on Mill St., 1864, painted by William Armstrong

brewer, as well as the Helliwells of Todmorden, whose grist mill near Pottery Road had been among the first in York and who subsequently opened the East End Brewery on River Street just north of Queen. Still later, there was Queen City Malting, just west of Berkeley Street, the huge Dominion Brewery on Lot just west of Sumach Street, the Lager Beer Brewery near Sherbourne Avenue, and the Reinhardt Brewery and Hotel on Mark Street near the Don River. Some of the brewers, particularly Gooderham and Worts, developed sidelines to their distilleries, such as fattening cattle on swill or spent mash. Large barns for the Gooderham and Worts cattle were located on Trinity Street.

With the presence of so many cattle, it was inevitable that in due course the distilling businesses would have as neighbours slaughterhouses like Thompson Flanegan & Brown, the Toronto Packing House, and Davies Meat Packing, later Canada Packers. Rendering plants, soap works like Morse Soap Company and the Toronto Soap Company, and tanners like A.R. Clark & Company are examples of only a few of the industries that grew up along the Lake and near the Don River. From bad water in the 1830s, to worse water in the 1880s, the stench in the area must have been overpowering as industry expanded near the mouth of the Don.

When the Gooderham and Worts windmill was erected in 1832, however, this commercial development was still in the future. Only the lands south of Queen Street had been released for sale, with funds to be used for a hospital. The rest of the Cabbagetown reserve was officially still called "The Park," and little of it was thought attractive for human settlement. The westward and northward growth of the city occurred first, and little attention was paid to the eastern blocks of the original townsite, still partly vacant.

Even so, as early as the 1820s, there were the beginnings of an Irish Catholic presence, manifest in the construction of the original St. Paul's Church north of King Street and east of Parliament. (Today's St. Paul's on Queen Street replaced the smaller church in the late 1880s.) By the early 1840s, another group of area residents — Irish Anglicans too poor to pay the high pew rates at St. James — sought and were granted their own

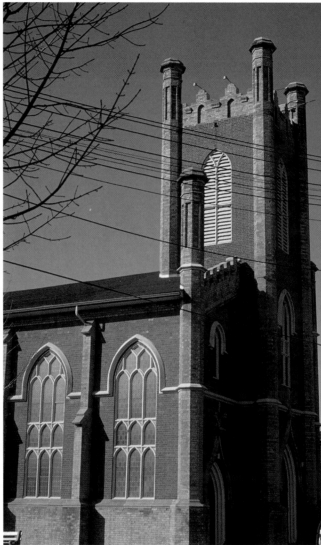

Little Trinity Church on King St. E.

its first — and for many years its only — co-educational school.

Around this small institutional cluster, an Irish community comprising both Catholics and Protestants swelled by the close of the 1840s. The failure of Ireland's potato crops, the enclosures of the time, and the refusal of the United States to take any but the healthiest of immigrants, led to a vast influx of poor, often ill immigrants to Canada. In 1847, when the population of Toronto was only about 21,000, over 38,500 Irish immigrants

parish. In 1843, Trinity Church — now known as Little Trinity — was built a block east of Parliament Street on the south side of King. The funds for its construction were provided primarily by the Gooderham and Worts families, suggesting that many of those served by the new church would have been in their employ. Soon after, Enoch Turner paid for construction of the small schoolhouse built adjacent to Little Trinity in 1847. It was unique in being not only the city's first free school, but

passed through the city. Close to 3,500 of these were admitted to the city's original General Hospital and almost 800 died, mainly of typhoid fever. Most of these immigrants were

Enoch Turner Schoolhouse on Trinity St.

expelled by city authorities to the countryside, where many more died, although some eventually found work and ultimately may even have prospered. By 1850, Toronto's population had increased by almost 50 percent to some thirty thousand. Most of the newcomers were Irish, and most of them settled along Queen Street or south, between Parliament and the Don River, close to the new industries that employed them.

Their original homes would not have been more than shacks, wooden frames covered with rough plaster. Maps of the 1850s, 1860s, and later indicate that lots were sometimes less than 4 metres wide, although 5 metre lots were more common. Often the homes were hardly larger

Wellesley cottages

Worts' family monument, St. James Cemetery

least forty-five. The police and later the fire department were mainly Orange, and the Order came to control municipal politics to a great extent well into the twentieth century.

Meanwhile, developments of a very different sort were underway at the north end of the Cabbagetown reserve. By 1850, two parcels of land, equivalent to almost an entire Park Lot, had been set aside for burial purposes. The larger, 26-hectare St. James Cemetery replaced the small plot adjacent to St. James Church on King Street. Originally the property of Governor Simcoe, the land just south of the Rosedale Ravine was deeded in 1845 to the Anglican Church by Bishop Strachan, and its elegant plan drawn up by the city's first architect,

than the privies behind them. After the fire of 1849, which levelled much of the developed area, the use of brick throughout Toronto became more common, but in the original Cabbagetown, brick would have been extremely rare. It is amazing that there were no major residential fires.

Whether the area was then known as Little Belfast or Corktown is not known. It *is* known that it was not called Cabbagetown before the 1880s, but it is certain that the religious animosities of Belfast, County Cork, and the rest of Ireland were rife. Many, if not most, of the original English and Loyalist residents of Toronto regarded Catholicism with suspicion. While Dr. William Warren Baldwin, at the time a reform-minded member of the provincial parliament, sought to ban the Orange Order as early as 1823, it flourished as an increasing number of potential combatants were crowded into this little enclave. The first Grand Lodge in the city was created in 1830, with another dozen lodges following during the course of the decade. In the 1840s, seventeen more lodges were created and by 1860, there were at

The Necropolis

Chapel of St. James-the-Less

The Necropolis

John G. Howard, who was later to bequeath High Park and his home, Colborne Lodge, to Torontonians. Cited frequently as one of the ten best-designed buildings in Canada, the 1858 gothic-styled Chapel of St. James-the-Less was designed by the firm of Cumberland and Storm. Buried in its cemetery are most of the Family Compact, the more plebeian Helliwells, the millers of Todmorden, Enoch Turner, most of the Gooderham and Worts clans, and Sir Casimir Gzowski, the engineer who built the Grand Trunk Railway.

Toronto's other early cemetery, Potter's Field, was located at the northwest corner of Bloor and Yonge Streets. As Yorkville grew, the cemetery impeded develop-

ment. So fifteen acres south and east of the St. James Cemetery, just north of Winchester and east of Sumach Streets, were set aside to serve as the non-sectarian burial grounds. The Necropolis — the city of the dead — was laid out just as St. James-the-Less was being completed. By 1877 those buried at the Yorkville site had all been moved, and the former Potter's Field became available for development. As at St. James, the Necropolis boasts a beautiful chapel designed by Henry Bower Lane, this one more romantic than gothic. Here, too, are buried many of Toronto's worthies, such as rebel William Lyon Mackenzie, George Brown, founder of the Toronto *Globe*, and Peter Rothwell Lamb, father of Daniel Lamb, the

something of the character that marked her reign. For the city, this was a decade of prosperity. The first railroads were built, with the Grand Trunk running right along the southern edge of the community. Toronto effectively became the gateway to the west, a function greatly enhanced by the completion of the canal linking Lakes Huron and Superior, which further expanded Great Lakes shipping.

For the residents of the embryonic Cabbagetown community, all the world-shattering advances of the era translated simply but importantly into a greater chance of finding work and improving their standard of living. *Boulton's Atlas* for 1858 shows that, by that year, the area south of King Street down to the Gooderham and Worts property had been subdivided and developed, particularly in the blocks near St. Paul's, Little Trinity, the Enoch Turner schoolhouse and the first publicly built school in the area, the original Park School. Some eight to

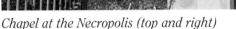
Chapel at the Necropolis (top and right)

alderman and philanthropist who helped found the Riverdale Zoo in the 1890s.

Although Victoria ascended to the throne in 1837, it was not until the 1850s that Toronto began to have

Toronto General Hospital on Gerrard St. E., about 1867

but it was not until 1854 that the project got underway when hospital trustees decided to construct a new hospital in the Cabbagetown Reserve. The site selected comprised 1.6 hectares on the north side of what was to become Gerrard, between Sackville and Sumach Streets. Completed in 1856, Toronto General Hospital was a very grand white-brick building with Mansard roofs. Originally built to accommodate 250 patients, it was expanded repeatedly and its wards were roomy, modern and well-ventilated.

Associated with the hospital were a host of other medical facilities including: the Burnside Lying-In Hospital, the Andrew Mercer Eye and Ear Infirmary, a dispensary for women, a convalescent home, and a mortuary. Toronto General Hospital acquired an excellent reputation in the medical world and was a major training facility. Its Toronto School of Medicine

ten blocks north of King Street, between the Don River and Sumach Street, also had been subdivided into very small lots, although buildings were not yet shown in *Boulton's Atlas*. There were a few small houses farther north and a few blocks that had been subdivided, but almost no rows or terraces were constructed. Larger houses in the northern reaches of the community were also few in number.

In addition, as is so often the case during periods of economic expansion, public spending increased. It had been evident since the first cholera plague of 1832 that the little Toronto General Hospital at King and Simcoe Streets was inadequate to serve the community. The sale of land south of Queen and east of Parliament Streets was to have provided funds for its replacement,

"Roselands," Samuel Ridout's house on Seaton St., in the 1860s

Victoria Skating Rink, Gerrard and Sherbourne St., 1863

eventually became the medical faculty of Victoria College. Trinity College Medical School operated out of 41 Spruce Street from 1871 to 1903. The Ontario Medical College for Women, located at 289 Sumach Street, was one of the first women's medical schools anywhere. It opened in 1883 and eventually became Women's College Hospital. Finally, there was a school of nursing, the second to open in Ontario

That these facilities were primarily for the poor and indigent can be gathered from the comments of C. Pelham Mulvany, M.D., who published a general guide to Toronto in 1882, which, not surprisingly, paid special attention to medical matters. In writing of admissions to the hospital, which required the personal approval of the Toronto Medical Health Officer, Dr. Canniff, he says:

Any reader of our city papers, in which the number of applicants and the number of admissions to the hospital, which Dr. Canniff has been able to grant each forenoon, must see how much of the difficulty of this difficult duty has been increased by the rapid influx of English and Irish pauperism, which has come upon us during the last ten years.

At that time, anyone of means who required extended care received it at home. The range and extent of med-

Postcard view of Don Jail, built 1865

ical facilities available to ordinary people was impressive, especially when one remembers that it was a period not particularly sympathetic toward the poor. Most other welfare services of the time were provided by the churches or benevolent societies, such as the Irish Protestant Benevolent Society, which built orphanages in the area, and the enormous Catholic House of Providence

Toronto School of Medicine on Gerrard St. E., about 1885

near St. Paul's Church, which served people of all denominations.

Another public purchase of the 1850s was 48 hectares of the land that once had been the Scadding Farm, for which the City paid £10,000. The intent of the acquisition was to establish a jail farm, but in the end, only the area where the Don Jail was built was used for penal purposes, and by 1890, the remainder of the Scadding property, along with some additional parcels added subsequently, became the 65-hectare Riverdale Park. In 1899, the Cabbagetown area alderman, Daniel Lamb, donated to the City a number of small birds and animals, which formed the nucleus of what became the Riverdale Zoo.

Presiding over the city's growth during the mid-1850s when the Grand Trunk Railroad came to town was Mayor George William Allan. Allan was the eleventh mayor of the city, and the first selected from St. David's Ward, which from 1847 through 1873 was bounded by Jarvis, Bloor, the Don, and Queen Street, thereby taking in what there then was of Cabbagetown. Allan, the son of the Honourable William Allan, inherited the family fortune including the Moss Park estate, one of the original Simcoe Park Lots, which then was also in St. David's Ward.

House of Providence, 1855

Riverdale Park, about 1900

A highly civic-minded businessman, Allan was better known for his extracurricular interests: the arts and floriculture. He served as president of the Ontario Society of Artists, and chairman of the Art Union of Canada, president of the Historical Society, the Upper Canada Bible Society, the Toronto Conservatory of Music, and the Royal Canadian Institute.

Riverdale Farm today

"Moss Park," William Allan's house on Sherbourne St., 1897

Alderman Daniel Lamb (left) and conductors, Winchester St., about 1899

His horticultural interests — for twenty-five years he was president of the Horticultural Society of Toronto — led him to donate 2 hectares of gardens to the city, which later was expanded to 6 hectares and today is known as Allan Gardens. A Fellow of the Royal Geographical Society and the Zoological Society, he travelled extensively, and in his Victorian fashion, collected specimens wherever he went. Today's Allan Gardens greenhouses, still remarkably Victorian, continue to reflect his

The interior of the Palm House at Allan Gardens

The Pavilion at Allan Gardens, 1895

diverse and eclectic interests, which in later life included becoming Speaker of the Canadian Senate and Chancellor of Trinity University.

Although it was just outside the geographical bounds of Cabbagetown, Allan Gardens played an important role in the life of the community. Not only was it among the most easily reached manicured parks — it pre-dated the formal portions of Riverdale Park by almost twenty years — the 1879 pavilion built within its gates was, until it burned down in 1902, the largest indoor public space in the city, providing Cabbagetowners with ready access to a key venue for public and political debate.

By 1860, the first period of railroad construction had passed, and Toronto, already a centre for commodities, had also become, irrevocably, a regional centre for transportation, manufacturing, and even finance. Still, the early 1860s were difficult, owing in large part to the

Toronto in the 1890s, looking northwest from Front St.

American Civil War, which slowed trade and growth in both countries. At its conclusion, however, the economy picked up, a trend that continued through the 1870s, reached its zenith — for Cabbagetown even more than for many other parts of Toronto — in the 1880s, slowed briefly during the 1890s, only to pick up again after 1900.

In fact, by 1873, the population of Cabbagetown was about 7,000 (in a city of about 56,000), sufficient to warrant its being made a city ward unto itself. Until 1891,

St. David's and Cabbagetown were one and the same — which undoubtedly helped give the area a sense of identity. Also helpful was the fact that the first mayor of Toronto after this readjustment of ward boundaries was Francis Henry Medcalf from the newly defined St. David's. A staunch Conservative and ardent Protestant, he was active in the Orange Order. One of eight children whose parents left Ireland in 1819, his father, a millwright and blacksmith, opened the Don Foundry and

Francis Medcalf

schools of the more populous southern portions of the area, industries even farther south and along the Don and up River Street, retail strips along Queen and King Streets with some retail movement up Parliament, and the subdivision of much of the remaining land into fairly small parcels.

From this point until about 1890, much of the remainder of the community was filled in. Small homes and cottages, some singly, but many in long rows, were built throughout the area. In general, construction moved northward from Queen. Larger homes, such as the two homes belonging to area builder Benjamin Brick at 314 and 308 Carlton, as well as many others along Carlton, Wellesley and Winchester, also were constructed during this period. The combination, at least in the northern part of the community, provided Cabbagetown with one of the features that continues to make it unique to this day: the proximity of the well-to-do and the less-well-to-do. Another feature of the community was that virtually all the post-1860 newcomers to the area were either native Canadians or of British extraction.

308 Carlton St.

Machine Shops, which despite burning down at least five times was very successful, permitting Medcalf, who was known as "Old Squaretoes," a reference to his work boots, to capitalize on his rags-to-riches story. Although popularly elected twice — in 1874 and 1875 — he does not seem to have been highly regarded by his political peers. His greatest contribution was said to be in getting the fire department up and running as a professional — and thoroughly Orange — service.

Thus at the start of the period of economic expansion that began in the mid-1860s, which of course included the arrival of more immigrants, the major features of Cabbagetown had been marked out — the cemeteries and potential park land to the north, the large hospital complex around Gerrard Street, the churches and

in 1859. By 1890, however, it had already ceased to be a school, having become part of the Cherry Street Hotel, but the other schools of the area (some now re-built, others original) also date from this major community-building period, namely Winchester (1874), Lord Dufferin (1876), Rose Avenue (1883) and Sackville (1887). Hotel Winchester opened in 1888 as the Lake View Hotel about a decade after some of the still-extant terraces along Parliament were built. (*See Tour One for more information about these buildings.*)

Toronto Dance Theatre, once St. Enoch's Church, on Winchester St.

With the homes came both public and private neighbourhood institutions. St. Enoch's (now Toronto Dance Theatre), St. Peter's , All Saints', St. Bartholomew's, St. Simon the Apostle, Sacré-Coeur, and the Berkeley Street Methodist Church, all date from the mid-1860s to 1890. In addition to Enoch Turner and Park Schools, the Palace Street School was constructed

St. Peter's Anglican Church, Carlton St.

Hotel Winchester, Parliament St.

But while the 1870s and 1880s run together in terms of overall conditions and the development of the community, there was in the 1870s still enough wild space to create a different character for the area. Writer Ernest Thomson Seton could still describe the Don River from the lakeshore up to Gerrard Street as:

A happy land of bosky hills and open meadows abounding in bobolinks; and meandering down between, among them, was the winding river and occasional ducks. Far away to the south and east were the marsh and the sandy bars of Toronto Bay.

And wind it did. A huge bend ran from the Winchester Street Bridge to Broadview Avenue, abutting the valley wall between Riverdale and Withrow Avenues, before swinging back across the Valley all the way to present-day Geneva Street. The Don was heavily used for recreational boating, for swimming and ice skating, and it was always described as picturesque. There were at least five islands in the River south of Bloor Street, and it flooded almost every spring as it had for centuries.

Writing at the close of the decade, historian Henry Scadding noted that from the 1790s onward, people had busily tried to fill in the marshy areas, and he reckoned that the attempts:

Show how the valley of the Don … will ultimately be turned to account, when the necessities of the population demand outlay. At present such improvements are discouraged by the length of time required to cover large surfaces of new clay with vegetable mold. But in future years it will be for mills and factories and not for suburban villa purposes.

Don River, about 1920

Note the use of the word *improvement*. By the 1880s, the spirit of Victorian reform, based on blind faith in progress, had taken hold in Toronto just as it had in Britain. One of its manifestations was a scheme to improve the Don so that it would run in a nice straight line to permit shipping, reduce flooding, and enable the land along its banks to be profitably used by industry.

The Don Improvement — as it was actually called — like many other reforms of the day was a hot political issue. The main argument, however, was over whether public money should be spent on the project. Few ques-

Don River today

Gooderham and Worts, 1896

tioned its merits. The idea for the project was an unintended result of the assassination of U.S. President Garfield who died in September 1881. For some unfathomable reason, Toronto's Mayor McMurrick attended the funeral in Cleveland, and while there was greatly impressed by the way in which the Cuyahoga River had been made to flow so as to meet the needs of industry.

Back in Toronto, a company was quickly formed by a number of honourable gentlemen, including at least one alderman, to undertake the project and lease the newly created land to industry. As well, a commitment seems to have been made to Canadian Pacific to permit it to run a track along the west side of the newly straightened river and to build a station at Queen Street. The project was advertised to the public as a method of improving sanitary conditions in the neighbourhoods adjacent to the River. In 1886, the Don Improvement was approved by the municipal electorate.

By 1891, the physical form of Cabbagetown was largely complete. Only the blocks around the General Hospital were to change radically in the first half of the twentieth century. The population of Cabbagetown in

1891 was more than 22,000, in a city that had climbed to 181,000. The numbers immediately after this year are difficult to obtain because Cabbagetown again became part of a larger ward, now called Ward II. By then, however, it clearly was a distinct community.

Alpha cottages, Geneva Ave.

Cottages, Trinity St.

Looking at some of Cabbagetown's smaller homes as they are today, such as the Wellesley Cottages or the neat rows on Geneva or Alpha Avenues, it is easy to think they must have been cozy and comfortable. But today's look is somewhat misleading; most of these houses have been improved far beyond their original condition. In the 1890s, many Cabbagetown houses, especially the older ones south of Gerrard Street, would have had at best brick facades. The remaining walls would either have been party walls, stucco, or wood covered with shingle or boards. They were drafty, few had central heating, most were heated by wood or coal — warm kitchens, cold bed-rooms — and fuel was often too expensive to obtain.

The area's industries were dirty and smelly, especially in the summer. Wood and coal fumes would have supple-mented both the dirt and the smells in the colder months. An 1885 analysis of housing throughout Toronto rated the entire area as containing third-class housing (fourth-class was the worst), although this was mainly because so many homes still were served by out-door privies. The houses themselves, after all, were not very old nor were they particularly badly built.

The last few decades of the century were inordinately fertile for inventors. Refrigerated trains, typewriters, elec-

Lamb & Co. Factory, 1890

tric lights, the telephone, bicycles, Daimler's automobile, and a host of other useful items poured out of workshops. Few, however, made much difference to Cabbagetowners.

The main exception was the streetcar, used mainly to get to work — it was too expensive for mere pleasure — and, until late in the century, not available on Sundays.

Bright St.

ing eventually to be able to send for their wives and children.

Cabbagetowners almost always arrived in the area as an intact family unit. They also had the advantage of already speaking the language of their new home. And they had strong institutions: formal ones like churches, schools and the Orange Order; and informal ones like the corner stores that gave credit. There undoubtedly was drunkenness — for much of the century beer and liquor were safer to drink than water — but as that changed, the number of pubs quickly fell from 493 serving a population of 68,000 in the mid-1870s, to 150, serving a population of 286,000 in 1906. And there do not seem to be reports of undue violence on the streets or in Cabbagetown homes.

The figures also suggest that, as the century progressed, home ownership in the neighbourhood was increasing and wealth, although meagre, was being slowly accumulated. In sum, Cabbagetown, by the end of the nineteenth century, was a predominantly working-class neighbourhood interspersed with some middle- to upper-middle-class homes. Its population was very conservative, quite orderly and probably quite optimistic about the coming century.

Modern conveniences inside the average Cabbagetown home were also rare. There were no refrigerators — the iceman came — and no washing machines — at best, a wringer. Families were larger then, so the bijou cottages admired today would have been quite crowded, and many held more than one family. Most of Cabbagetown's workers were unskilled or semi-skilled. As a result, they were among the last hired and the first fired. When they did work, the six-day work week ran to fifty or sixty hours.

On the other hand, much was good about Cabbagetown. Although it was poor, it was not a slum. It was a far cry from the scene many had left behind in England, such as the London described by Mayhew or the Manchester described by Engels. Unlike even Toronto's "Ward" — the area north of city hall — it was a neighbourhood of families. In the Ward, as in many slums, men often arrived in the new world alone, hop-

The Ward, about 1912

3
THE TWENTIETH CENTURY

Parliament St. at Dundas St., about 1932

The twentieth century has not been easy for Cabbage-town. It started well, but even before the onset of World War I in 1914, a depression that might well have had devastating consequences for the community was underway. The war that interrupted that depression took the lives of many of the area's young men. A socially, psychologically, and financially frantic decade followed the war's conclusion, but the worst was yet to come.

The Great Depression, hard for almost everyone, was particularly destructive for Cabbagetown, with its mainly working-class residents and stock of poorly built, aging housing. World War II brought jobs, but as with World War I, also death and certainly no improvement to the physical fabric of the community. The much-vaunted prosperity of the post-World War II period led to a well-intentioned war on poverty that for Cabbagetown meant the planned destruction of the heart of the neighbourhood and its replacement first by the public housing of Regent Park and, later, the less-well-intentioned private housing of St. Jamestown. Fortunately, people began to question the merits of these "improvements," and banded together to find a more humane way of dealing with the

Metcalfe St.

area's deterioration. The last quarter of the century has been an "up" period, one in which the community has taken back its heart and soul.

The future, too, looks bright. The neighbourhood is being spruced up, a sensitive re-development of the Gooderham and Worts site is underway; there has been much attention to ecologically correct repair of the River valley, and there are even plans to improve Regent Park.

The Edwardian Era

If ever a period deserved to be called the age of optimism, it was the years between the turn of the century and the outbreak of World War I. Everything the late Victorians believed and practised regarding progress and the improvability of humankind seemed to be bearing fruit; it

Women's Dispensary on Seaton St., 1914

may also have been the only time for which "trickle-down economics" bore at least some relation to reality.

Toronto was booming. In 1891, its population accounted for only 8.6 percent of those living in Ontario; by 1901, the percentage had reached 9.5, climbing to 14.9 by 1911, and 17.8 in 1921. Toronto's population, which was 208,000 in 1901, was 376,500 by 1911 and was to reach 521,000 by 1921. These figures were accounted for by a combination of inmigration, natural increase, and annexation. The value of manufactured products grew between 1901 and 1911 from some $58 million to almost $155 million, while the value of building permits in the same period went from $3.5 million to $24 million, climbing to over $27 million in both 1912 and 1913. Every other indicator tracked during those years — city assessments, bank clearings, and mortality — reflected the same pattern. From being merely a regional financial centre, Toronto had emerged as a strong continental centre, behind New York, Boston and Montreal as far as Europe was concerned, but vying with Chicago for western business.

Public health was improving as provision was made for clean water and adequate sewage disposal and treatment. By the end of World War I, backyard privies had been virtually eliminated, replaced by indoor plumbing. Vaccination was widespread and there were well-baby clinics, public nurses, and pasteurized milk. As a result, the death rate per thousand dropped from 15.18 in 1896 to 11.20 in 1914, a stunning improvement. Also during this period, consumer products like meat began to be inspected. The *Toronto Star*, a progressive crusading paper published by Joe Atkinson, regularly published the addresses of dairies and markets deemed safe by the public health officer, enabling consumers to make educated choices about where they bought their food. In 1912, the paper sponsored a fly-swatting contest, it having become clear that these pesky insects were the source of many ailments. The contest had to be called off, however, when it was discovered that some people were breeding flies in order to kill them!

This was also the period when great institutions of culture were established. Music emerged first, with the founding of the Mendelssohn Choir and the construction of Massey Hall, both in the 1890s. By the early twentieth century, the Art Gallery of Ontario, the Royal Ontario Museum, and the Royal Alexandra Theatre had also been founded. Toronto may only have been Canada's second city, but the University of Toronto was by far the largest

Sunnyside, one of many amusement parks, in the 1920s

in the country. In addition to the ever-popular Canadian National Exhibition and the Toronto Islands, places of amusement intended for the masses began to rise — Sunnyside's pavillions, the Beaches' amusement parks, the gardens and zoo at Riverdale Park, and mineral baths — a process that continued through the 1920s.

The growth, progress, reform, commitment to beautification, and sheer energy of this era did not suddenly vault Cabbagetowners into the ranks of the middle class. On the contrary, the area remained a working-class enclave, but at least its residents had work. True, another fire in 1904 destroyed a large portion of downtown Toronto, no doubt wiping out hundreds of low-paying jobs of the sort Cabbagetowners tended to hold, but the area's reconstruction, including the construction of Toronto's first skyscrapers, created hundreds of new jobs,

and the new pressurized water system and improved fire-fighting capacity of the city no doubt saved many lives and much property.

Inflation during the early twentieth century greatly diminished the value of increased earnings, but growing home ownership in Cabbagetown — as elsewhere in the city — and rising assessment values, demonstrate that for residents of the community, things were getting better, however slightly. During this period, however, Cabbagetown lost one of its major institutions. The Toronto General Hospital which had stood on Gerrard Street between Sackville and Sumach Streets was replaced by the new, larger, more modern facility that still stands on the south side of College Street, just east of University Avenue. With the hospital, went all the ancillary facilities: the lying-in hospital, the women's dis-

Wellington St., after the fire of 1904

Spruce Court, about 1920

pensary (which moved to the far west end on Rusholme Road) and the three medical faculties. The hospital building was used during World War I for wounded soldiers, but was demolished in the 1920s. The Women's Medical College and Trinity Medical School buildings still stand, having been converted to housing.

Attitudes, always slower to change, also began to shift in this period. The poor, so frequently scorned and blamed for their own misfortune, helped begrudgingly if at all, and only if they were "deserving," began to be perceived as a possible threat, people who might organize themselves into unions or be attracted to radical politics. And perhaps for a few of the more enlightened, there was a more sophisticated understanding of the economics, as opposed to the supposed morality, of poverty. Whatever the reasons, under the urging of the city's Public Health Officer, Dr. Charles Hastings, the Toronto Housing Company was formed by the city and various philanthropists. Under the direction of businessman and realtor

George Frank Beer, the company's president, two projects were completed just before World War I: Riverdale Court (now the Bain Avenue Co-op) on the east side of the Don River, and Spruce Court in Cabbagetown.

Armistice Day, 11 November 1918, on King St.

Swimmers in the Don River, about 1920

Both projects were based on the Garden City model, a form promoted most vigorously by Ebenezer Howard of England as the only sure means of building moral character as well as solving the housing shortage. As Howard promised, both projects have been well-maintained and provide their residents with a strong sense of community. In fact, the design by outstanding residential architect Eden Smith became a model for much middle-class housing throughout North America, especially after World War II. Unfortunately, it ceased to serve as a prototype for later public projects like Regent Park.

Although immigrants to Toronto in this period increasingly came from parts of Europe other than the British Isles — those of Anglo-Saxon origin comprised 91.7 percent of the city's population in 1901, but only 86.4 percent of the total a decade later — Cabbagetown itself continued to be almost uniformly British and, in fact, from the 1870s on, newcomers to Cabbagetown were almost all English as Irish immigration fell off. The new residents' loyalty to England was deeply ingrained — the Boer War, for example, was warmly supported in Toronto — and although precise numbers are not available, it is a safe assumption that a somewhat disproportionate number of the 70,000 men from Toronto who enlisted to fight in World War I came from Cabbagetown. Of this total, 10,000 did not return.

Carlton St.

After World War I

Of the 60,000 who did return, a fair proportion had been physically or psychologically wounded. In fact, whether it was the horror, discomfort, or sheer boredom of that particular war, all western culture seems to have suffered irreparably in its aftermath.

Up until the Great Depression, the economy was fair: it had its ups and downs, but it never regained the pace of real growth that occurred before the war. Instead, there were the frantic stock market gyrations of the late 1920s. Women got and exercised the vote, social behaviour became more relaxed, there were more leisure-time activities like movies and amusement parks, unions made inroads into working life, talk of political change was rampant, but every advance was counterbalanced by crackdowns on anything that smacked of radicalism or foreignness. No one seemed able to recapture the pre-war optimism. The period is sometimes called "The Roaring Twenties," but really it seems to have been more like a prolonged silent scream, an unsettled age, and although voluble Cabbagetowners lived through it — Gordon Sinclair and Hugh Garner among them — none spoke of it as the period that shaped or moved them. That came with the Great Depression.

The Dirty Thirties

By 1929, the year of the phenomenal stock market crash that heralded the long Depression, Toronto's population was over 600,000. Writing of its character at the time, J.E. Middleton, official historian of Toronto's 1934 centennial, assessed it as "a Tory city," populated by Irish, English, and Scottish immigrants.

And what was true of Toronto could also be said of

Cabbagetown, which apart from a minuscule group of Macedonians and Jews in the Regent Park area, continued to be even more predominantly British than most other parts of a city that was still 85 percent Anglo-Saxon.

It also continued to be poor. Although poverty was the hallmark of most inner-city neighbourhoods in the 1930s, Cabbagetown was particularly hard hit. Its working-class residents were not working. Its stock of housing was ageing; the southern and central portions of the community were now between sixty and ninety years old, and there was no money for any of the repairs even a well-built house of that age would require. Families doubled up, took in boarders or, more frequently, lost their homes and became tenants. The northern, generally newer and better-built portion of Cabbagetown was not immune to this decline. These homes — many fifty or sixty years old — were also ageing and deteriorating. Their owners, too, were pinched, doubling up, taking in boarders or losing their homes outright. Many of the larger homes along Carlton and Winchester Streets, as well as on Jarvis Street and Sherbourne Avenue, became rooming houses in the 1930s. Some remain rooming houses to this day.

Cabbagetown became almost a curse word. Having to move there

Cabbagetown house and garden, 1936

was considered by those who lived elsewhere to be akin to going to hell. Only the area around today's City Hall, which was known as "The Ward," was thought worse. Its squalor could be justified in the minds of most Torontonians, however, by the fact that it was full of for-

eigners. Something of the bitterness and bewilderment that must have been widespread throughout the period was voiced later by author Hugh Garner in an interview that appeared in *The Tamarack Review* in 1969:

Cabbagetown had one unique feature which has amazed some people who haven't given it any thought. It happened to be the largest Anglo-Saxon slum in North America … we were all English and Scots; we all belonged to the Anglican or Presbyterian churches; we were the establishment except that we were the freak-outs from the establishment. The foreigners, the immigrants, would come here and think, "If I were only English I could be president of the Bank of Commerce." And here we were, we were as English as you could get, and sang in the Anglican choir and everything else, and we lived in a slum.

Poverty in the 1930s had a different feel from poverty today, or perhaps even of an earlier time. The condition was so

Sumach St.

widespread as to seem a worldwide plague, rather than a punishment visited on a few miscreants. But physically, it was even more devastating than poverty today.

Depression was an apt term in more ways than one. The overwhelming sense one gets of the period is of men huddled on grey street corners, of not-quite-clean children grubbing for fuel to heat dilapidated houses, of

garbage blowing along desolate streets. The services cities had begun to provide such as health care and garbage collection, to say nothing of beautification, became unaffordable. In Tory Toronto, there was little of the radicalism of the Prairies, but still, as the Depression wore on, there was some relief as Canada's cities and provinces prevailed on the federal government to provide some funds for welfare, some work for wages, some money for household repairs.

For Cabbagetown, perhaps the only saving grace during this era was the great green lung of the Don Valley. There, some of the poor encamped from time to time in tent cities. There, too, children and adults could ramble, dream, and play with a fair degree of safety, and also from time to time, there were organized amusements that even the poorest could afford.

The real turning point, however, was World War II. Finally, there was something for men to do. Again, Cabbagetown sent a disproportionate number of its young off to the war. At home, there was now work for women and those who could not fight. There were few noticeable improvements to Cabbagetown — or anywhere else — during World War II, but there was a reason for the daily difficulties and sacrifices. And for the first time in over a decade, there was again hope for the future.

After World War II

The aftermath of World War II presents a stark contrast to the period that followed the first war, when people sought to return to the century's early optimism and failed utterly. After 1945, there was an almost obsessive desire to embrace the new, to start afresh, to avoid at any cost anything old fashioned, especially a return to the Depression of the 1930s. Anyone who lived through the Depression, or grew up with parents who experienced it, will know how deeply scarring and frightening the experience proved. It seems to have been regarded with more horror than the war.

No one, however devoted to future growth, stability and prosperity, could possibly have predicted just how prosperous the post-World War II period was to be. Along with the rest of North America, Toronto boomed. Couples who had postponed having children because of the Depression and then the War began having families. Suburbs mushroomed. Consumerism ran rampant. Radio, then television, changed people's recreational activities, and ultimately, their perceptions of the world. From an initial refusal to accept any immigrants other than English war brides, it became evident, by 1951, when unemployment stood at 1.3 percent even though a full third of women had remained in the workforce, that immigrants were absolutely necessary. And so the floodgates were opened.

One area that continued to lag behind through the 1950s was

Dundas St. E., 1951

housing. Suburban homes were being built fast and furiously, but not fast enough to meet the demand. Overcrowding throughout the inner city had become more of a problem rather than less, and meanwhile, the existing overburdened stock of housing had continued to deteriorate. Cabbagetown was in particularly bad shape. One of the key indicators of the health of neighbourhoods is the health of their residents and, by this measure, Cabbagetown was in trouble.

From its inception, the city's Department of Public Health had collected statistics on various aspects of health, among them birth and death rates, including infant mortality, still-birth, tuberculosis and maternal death rates, and finally, the rate of communicable diseases. Although statistics were not collected specifically for Cabbagetown since it was part of the Moss Park District, the whole area was similar enough socio-economically and in terms of its housing stock, infrastructure, and institutions to provide a revealing picture.

In 1951, the district led the city in its birth rate: 24.9 per 1,000 (the citywide rate was 21.1, the next highest district was Parkdale at 24.7). It also led in its death rate: 14.6 per 1,000 (the city rate was 11.6, precisely the rate for the second highest district, University). It led too with its infant mortality rate: 38.8 per 1,000 (the citywide rate was 25.2, the second highest district was Runnymede with 27). For stillbirths, Moss Park was the second highest district (the city rate was 1.9, the highest was Hillcrest with 2.5). Its tuberculosis death rate per 100,000 was again the highest in the city at 32.2 (the citywide rate was 6.2, while the lowest district was Yorkville, with only 3.5). Oddly, the maternal death rate was

Oak St., 1949

the second *lowest* in the city. At half the citywide rate of 1.2 per 100, Moss Park tied with Runnymede and the East End at .6. Only Yorkville with a maternal death rate of 0 was lower, while at the other extreme, in Riverdale, the rate was 3.6. Finally, for acute communicable diseases, the Moss Park District rate per 100,000 was again second highest at 6.4 (the city rate was 4.3, while the highest, Runnymede, at 9.2, was at that time an area of extremely high immigration of displaced persons who had spent years in refugee camps).

In short, while many other areas of the city were hit by one or two distressful aspects of poor health, Cabbagetown suffered from almost all of them. It was information like this that lent weight to what was readily observable: the area was in need of wholesale improvement. It was

Regent Park, 1949

Regent Park

"The Citizens' Housing and Planning Association," whose membership included a number of University of Toronto professors of social work and planning, but — not surprisingly — no neighbourhood members. The group prevailed upon Toronto's City Council to place a question on the ballot in the January 1947 election asking whether voters were in favour of financing the construction of Regent Park North at a cost of $5.9 million.

The measure passed by a resounding 30,000 to 18,000 votes. The project that ultimately was built contained 1,056 units and cost $16 million ($1.4 million of which came from the federal government, $1.3 million from provincial coffers) and required an additional vote of approval from the citizenry in 1952. Regent Park North was built between 1947 and 1957, and Regent Park South, which contained an additional 732 units, was completed in 1960.

Although it is relatively easy with the hindsight of almost fifty years to find fault with various key elements of Regent Park — the destruction of all commercial uses, the demolition of community institutions like churches, the closure of all through streets, the replacement of single-family homes with apartments — there is no denying that initially the project was a success. The

also this kind of medical and health data that had been collected in the nineteenth century by progressive-minded people to argue in favour of all manner of urban improvements. Slums were thought of in medical terms — as "the infernal wen," a blight, a cancer that was spreading — and the solutions offered were medical. The sore had to be cut out, the wound cleansed. The idea of starting entirely afresh, however, of re-inventing the very pattern of cities, although first articulated in the late nineteenth century, was not to flower in Canada until the post-World War II era. Unfortunately for Cabbagetown, it was to serve as the "patient" for a number of these experimental urban "treatments."

As early as 1932, a proposal was made for redevelopment of the area bounded by Sackville, Sumach, Dundas, and Oak Streets. Much like the scheme that eventually was built, this proposal closed off all the little streets that ran through the site and replaced the single-family houses which had lined those streets with a number of apartment blocks set amidst large patches of grass. As World War II drew to a close, the new style of planning gained popularity and became the rallying point for a group that called itself

Three Corners Co-op at Winchester St. and Metcalfe St.

units and rooms were new, clean, sun-filled, and large, replacing dark, dilapidated, overcrowded, unrepaired, ill-heated hovels. To the credit of the planners, the logistics of construction were such that all the existing residents of the area were re-housed in the new units; no one was displaced. When the project was completed, five thousand additional families were already on the waiting list.

The apparent success of the Regent Park development led to similar projects throughout Canada. But variations in the process and the outcome were introduced that made these less likely to succeed even from the outset. At nearby Moss Park, for example, the new buildings were entirely high-rises, a form inappropriate for families, although families were housed there. At Alexandra Park, in the Spadina-Dundas area south of Kensington Market,

Carlton St. (top and above)

homes in which their owners took great pride were expropriated at far below their replacement value, leading to anger and hardship. A similar process was followed with Don Mount, to the east of Cabbagetown. In both these projects, the areas' original occupants were displaced. With Trefann Court, to the south of Regent Park, there was no intention of housing low-income groups at all. Rather, the site being expropriated by the City was to be turned over to the private sector to develop middle-class town houses.

Finally, there were completely private ventures, such as St. Jamestown, where developers — aided and abetted by city re-zoning — practised a private form of expropriation that came to be called blockbusting. By purchasing a few houses and then filling them with the most unsavoury tenants imaginable, developers were able to drive prices down and cheaply acquire large blocks of land for profitable redevelopment that replaced the poor and working class with the more upwardly mobile.

Strengthening the Community

By the mid-1960s, these activities had begun to spur a backlash against both public housing and private redevelopment. Throughout what remained of Cabbagetown, people — whether middle or working class — felt extremely threatened. At the same time, it was becoming apparent to an ever-growing number that cities could not be saved by destroying them. The result was that residents began to strengthen community ties and to get organized politically. Out of the struggles in Don Vale, the area east of Parliament and north of Gerrard, a mixed-income neighbourhood threatened by blockbusting, came a sympathetic, reform-minded alderman, Karl Jaffary.

Sumach St.

Meanwhile, out of the anti-City Hall struggles in the Trefann Court area, came John Sewell. Sewell was also active in the area south of St. Jamestown, an area originally more like Don Vale socio-economically and physically, but which thanks to blockbusting was rapidly deteriorating.

One of many gardening centres in Cabbagetown

By the municipal election of 1972, these politicians and others like Bill Kilbourn and David Crombie had succeeded in persuading enough Torontonians that all was not well at City Hall. The old guard was thrown out. The blockbusters ceased to have the City's support, which greatly reduced the threat they posed to neighbourhoods all over the city. In addition, from that point on, a new, more sensitive approach was taken to publicly built housing, resulting in the innovative mixed-income St. Lawrence neighbourhood, and in the growth of co-ops and City Home projects in Cabbagetown.

Calling off the blockbusters resulted in largely unanticipated, significant changes to the remaining northern

St. Jamestown

portions of Cabbagetown on both sides of Parliament Street. No longer safe for large-scale developers, the area became a haven for the so-called "white painters" of the middle and upper-middle classes. With great vigour and much creativity, the yuppies of the 1970s and 1980s moved in, renovating homes and transforming workers' cottages

and mansions alike into Victorian showplaces. So active were their horticultural efforts that today virtually every corner store in the community boasts a garden centre.

Things were not so happy for Regent Park. To at least the same degree that the northern part of the community prospered, the central portion that had been its heart

Parliament St.

Windmill at Riverdale Farm

declined. The project's original occupants may have been delighted with their new homes, but try as many residents did to forge a community within the development, they never succeeded, and for later tenants, it was just another public housing project, with all the stigmas and discomforts attendant on such schemes. The design of the project — neither urban nor suburban — segregated it from the rest of Cabbagetown and, indeed, from the rest of the city.

Sometimes the proximity of these two areas has inspired creativity: Parliament Street has emerged as one of the most unusual shopping areas in the city, where thrift and junk shops are located cheek by jowl with trendy restaurants, bakeries and boutiques. More often, they represent two solitudes — not of ethnicity, but of class.

Wildflowers near the Don River

Into the Next Millennium

Luckily, the Cabbagetown story does not end here. Like any healthy, living organism, change is the community's only constant. One of the areas that struck people as being most in need of change was the Don Valley.

The late 1980s, when concern for the environment was at a peak, spawned a group called the Task Force to Bring Back the Don. Working as an advisory committee to City Council, the Task Force is almost entirely composed of ordinary citizens with a special interest in reviving the Valley and making amends for some of the damage done to it during the first two-hundred years of human settlement. Together with hundreds of volunteers, the group has planted close to thirty thousand trees in the Valley, returned dozens of hectares to a more natural state by planting wildflowers in place of mowed grass, developed informative materials for schools and the general public, worked with other agencies to get rid of the weirs that prevented fish

Don River

from migrating upstream, created new access points and, most ambitiously, created the award-winning Chester Springs Marsh to shelter wildlife and water-cleansing plants. Plans for the future include re-introducing meanders in the Don's path and creating an even larger marsh near the mouth of the river.

The Task Force is also working with the Riverdale Farm's board of directors to re-naturalize the ponds at the bottom of the Farm. The Farm itself provides an interesting story. When the Riverdale Zoo, which originally opened in the late 1890s, was replaced in the 1970s by the new Metro Zoo, Cabbagetown residents prevailed on the City to turn it into a farm rather than simply an ordinary park. Since its inception, the idea was that it should be a working farm, not a petting zoo. Gradually, the Farm has made a specialty of keeping and breeding rare and endangered nineteenth-century domestic breeds of sheep, pigs, cattle, and fowl.

Parliament St. shopping

The next area up for renewal is the oldest part of Cabbagetown, its most southern region. Construction has already begun to bring the 6-hectare Gooderham and Worts site back to life. Forty-five of the fine stone and brick buildings that were part of the distilling business — for generations, the largest in the British Empire — are slated for restoration or renovation for a great variety of uses ranging from markets and museums, to condominiums and co-ops, to industrial space geared primarily to film production and the businesses that support it.

Finally, too, the heart of Cabbagetown that was destroyed to create Regent Park is slated for major changes. Starting modestly with the area bound by Sumach, River, Gerrard, and Oak Streets, plans developed with extensive input from Regent Park residents are underway to knit the area back into the fabric of Toronto. In this first area, the old streets will be brought back, public housing buildings will be demolished to be replaced by houses and other buildings that face the street, and stores will again line Gerrard Street. There is to be a mixture of income groups and a variety of tenure types — private homes, rental units, co-ops, and possibly even condos, just as in the rest of Cabbagetown.

And so, like the modest vegetable for which it is named, Cabbagetown keeps gaining new and complex layers. A thriving community, Cabbagetown continues to evolve, changing with the times and adapting to the conditions of the day.

4
TWO WALKING TOURS

Tour One: Quintessential Cabbagetown

Tour One: Quintessential Cabbagetown

The nice thing about walking through northern Cabbagetown is that you can meander for hours through an almost purely Victorian neighbourhood. Rarely will you find a home or church less than a century old; commercial buildings vary more greatly in age, but a fair number have also reached the century mark.

The difficult thing about a walk through northern Cabbagetown is that if you want to spend less than a lifetime visiting every site of interest, it is hard to know where to start. The tour described here provides an opportunity to appreciate Cabbagetown's variety. It wanders past some notable churches, schools, and parks, along the community's "high street," and past both grand homes and modest cottages.

Allan Gardens (1)
Set amidst a 5-hectare city park, much of it a gift from nineteenth-century businessman and politician George

The Palm House

Allan, is a gracious 1910 glass-domed pavilion — the Palm House — connected to six greenhouses. In true Victorian style, today's botanical collection contains specimens gathered from around the globe, grouped according to temperature and moisture requirements rather than genus or geography.

Walk east on Carlton past Sacré-Coeur, one of Toronto's few French congregations, and St. Peter's Anglican Church, built in 1865.

165-179 Carlton St.

The Chamberlin Block, 165-179 Carlton Street (2)
From the 1860s through the early 1890s, Charles Chamberlin assembled land in the area and built stylish, solid commercial and residential buildings.

181-183, 185, 187-189 Carlton Street (3)
The two doubles were also the work of Charles Chamberlin. The westerly pair was built in 1878, the easterly in 1892. Chamberlin would probably have liked to pick up the property between them at 185 as well, but

it was already occupied by another home built between 1860 and 1865 for lumber dealer William Jamieson.

At Parliament Street, turn south.

181-183 Carlton St.

35 Spruce St.

35 Spruce Street (4)

Built in 1861, this home was for many years the residence of the dean of nearby Trinity College Medical School, but its original owner was Charles B. Mackay, a clerk at the old Front Street Customs House.

Trinity Mews

Trinity Mews, 41 Spruce Street (5)

From its construction in 1871 until 1903, this handsome red and yellow brick building housed Trinity Medical School. In the latter year, Trinity became part of the University of Toronto's Faculty of Medicine. The building served a variety of uses until it joined the partially new, upscale Trinity Mews complex.

Spruce Court Apartments, 74-86 Spruce Street (6)

Built in 1913, these Tudoresque units by architect Eden Smith are an early and excellent example of the classic garden apartment style that gained favour across North America in the 1940s and 1950s. They were built for the Toronto Housing Corporation, the first government-sponsored housing built in Canada.

Spruce Court Apartments

Site of Toronto General Hospital, Spruce Street (7)

The entire 1.5-hectare area between Sackville and Sumach Streets south of Spruce Street to Gerrard was from 1866 until 1914 the site of Toronto General Hospital. In 1921, the vacated hospital was demolished, and the houses on Gifford and Nasmith were built within the decade.

Continue east on Spruce. Turn south on Sumach.

Ontario Medical College for Women, 289 Sumach Street (8)

Dr. Emily Howard Jennings Stowe, a Quaker who had obtained an M.D. in New York in 1867, founded the Ontario Medical College for Women in 1883. In 1890, this rather grand Romanesque Revival edifice by Smith & Gemmel, opened its doors. Today the building is a ten-unit condo.

Turn north on Sumach.

wide meander brought it right to the foot of the hill at this point — and the Don Jail opposite. Originally, much of the park land you see was part of Scadding Estate, a portion of which later became the Jail's farm.

289 Sumach St.

397 Carlton St.

397 Carlton Street (10)

The street here is still paved in red brick, strengthening the image of elegant late Victorian living on a dignified street overlooking a gracious park with formal gardens. The first home, number 397, was built in an Italianate style in 1883 for barrister James Reeve. The double at 419-421 followed later the same year.

Geneva Street (9)

Both sides of this short street are lined with two-storey, mansard-roofed, mid-1880s workers' cottages, a type known as "Alpha," which succeeded an earlier peak-roofed style. Head north along the lane at the east end of Geneva Street to Carlton. From here, a sweeping view of the Don Valley can be enjoyed. Before the river was straightened in the 1880s, a

Geneva Street

Riverdale Park and Farm (11)

In the 1850s, the City of Toronto began acquiring land on both sides of the Don River, primarily from the Scadding Estate. From this land were carved the St. James and Necropolis Cemeteries. Much of the remainder was reserved for parks. In the 1890s, area alderman Daniel Lamb

Riverdale Farm

launched a fundraising drive to build the Riverdale Zoo. Adjacent to the Zoo were lovely formal gardens, and inside, along with the animals, the romantic Donnybrook Pavilion, donated by the Toronto Street Railway and still partially standing. When the Metro Zoo opened in 1978, Riverdale Zoo was converted to a farm, which now specializes in nineteenth-century domestic animals and plants. The farm-appropriate buildings on the site were all added later, some moved from elsewhere and others designed to look as though they had always been there.

384 Sumach Street (12)
Oddly, one of the most Victorian-looking houses in Cabbagetown is also one of its oldest. Built in 1866, it gained its Victorian charm only gradually, having been greatly altered over the years. For reasons that remain undetermined — even by the historian who has long owned and lovingly restored it — the house is known locally as the "Witch's House."

From Riverdale Park, head north across Winchester.

384 Sumach St.

Necropolis Cemetery and Chapel (13)
Laid out in 1858 to provide a "non-sectarian" (multi-denominational) burial ground, this "City of the Dead" contains the markers and remains of some of Toronto's most colourful characters, including William Lyon Mackenzie, leader of the 1837 Rebellion, and rebellion participants Samuel Lount and Peter Mathews, both of whom were

Necropolis

hanged for their part in the uprising. The charming 1872 chapel and gate house were designed by architect Henry Langley.

Head back west along Winchester.

Daniel Lamb House, 156 Winchester Street (14)
Portions of this house, set well back from the street, were built between 1830 and 1840. Subsequent changes vastly altered the building. The facade visible today dates from 1877. The home's most famous occupant was Alderman Daniel Lamb, son of the owner of the most northerly industry in Cabbagetown (see Hillcrest Park, below) and a popular politician credited with successfully promoting the creation of the Riverdale Zoo in the late 1890s.

Enter what seems a very secret and private place far from the bustling city by continuing west on Winchester then south on Sackville to a tiny lane, Sackville Place.

156 Winchester St.

Sackville Place (15)

Houses along Sackville Place, Woodstock Place, Bowman and Flagler Streets, date from the 1880s and were built on small lots directly abutting the street.

Head south on Bowman Street to Carlton Street.

Sackville Place

Benjamin Brick Home, 314 Carlton Street (16)

In the last quarter of the nineteenth century, the peak period of Cabbagetown's development, Carlton was incontestably the best address in the neighbourhood. Another of the area's builders, aptly named "Brick," built this home for himself in 1874. In 1890, he built himself a new home down the street at 308.

314 Carlton St.

288 Carlton St.

1886 double at 282-280 boasts some of the most decorative, gingerbread-like woodwork in the area, making it a favourite among TV commercial producers.

Metcalfe Row Houses, 1-25, 6-13 Metcalfe Street (18)

Many think of this as the most urbane street in Cabbagetown. Consisting of four separate rows: the odd-numbered ones (1-15, 17-25) built by Thomas Bryce in 1888-89 in a modified Queen Anne style, boast sizable quantities of stained glass; the even ones (6-18, 20-32) were built in 1883 and 1886 respectively.

10 Metcalfe St.

James L. Morrison House, 37 Metcalfe Street (19)

Definitely a house of many parts, and a tangled history. In 1875, a Captain John T. Douglas built a north-facing

37 Metcalfe St.

farmhouse-style home. Businessman James Morrison became its third owner in 1882. In 1891, he expanded the house and added a vast number of Italiante details. A subsequent owner sold the front lawn for the apartment house now at the corner of Winchester and Metcalfe, stripped the details that became hidden

Carlton Street, Sackville to Metcalfe Streets (17)

The best examples of Cabbagetown's many styles are contained within this short strip. Their original owners were the *crème de la crème* of local society. On the north side, at 300-298 and 296-294, are two fine 1889 Queen Anne doubles, often called "Bay-n-Gables." At 288 stands the very formal 1881 Second Empire residence of patent medicine merchant William Lumbers to which there is now attached a very formal c. 1880s Second Empire garage. Hugh Neilsen, a telephone company executive who had one of the earliest residential phones in Toronto, lived nearby in the 1878 Victorian Gothic pile at 295. The

by the new building and stuck them on the west side, which became the front of the house.

85 Winchester St.

At Sackville Street, head north toward Wellesley Street.

459-461 Sackville Street (22)

Most of the houses in this stretch were built between 1888 and 1891, except the one at the rear of 435, which dates from 1856. At Amelia is a corner store with an unusual wooden canopy that dates from the building's construction in 1888.

Walk north to Wellesley Street, then east.

St. Enoch's Presbyterian Church

St. Enoch's Presbyterian Church, 80 Winchester Street (20)

A vaguely Romanesque church, St. Enoch's is notable more for its varied history than its architecture. An early pastor was the Reverend Alexander MacMillan, father of musician Sir Ernest MacMillan, conductor of the Toronto Symphony Orchestra from 1931-56. Today it is the Toronto Dance Theatre and School.

Charles Parsons House, 85 Winchester Street (21)

Across the street and just east of St. Enoch's is another of the area's few pre-1870 homes. Built in 1857 for a leather merchant, it is one of the few from the period that still looks much as it did originally.

459-461 Sackville St.

419-421 Wellesley St.

419-421, 423 Wellesley Street (23)

Charles Scadding, an engraver, built the double. His widow, in an unusual move for the time, called in some architects to design the home at 423 in 1886 — most of Cabbagetown was built by builder-developers who did their own design work.

Hillcrest Park (24)

The southern portion of Wellesley Park at the east end of Wellesley Street was the site of the P.R. Lamb Manufactory. Founded in 1848, it made products like glue and stove blacking. The area had so

Hillcrest Park

changed by the time the factory burned in 1888 that it is unlikely such a noxious industry would have been tolerated much longer. For over a decade the park has hosted the annual Cabbagetown Forsythia Festival.

Wellesley Avenue (25)

All but two of the houses on this little street were built in 1887 by another builder active in the area, Frank Armstrong. Armstrong also built many of the much grander architect-designed homes in Toronto's Annex, and had an unusually fine eye for "off-the-rack" (prefabricated) building details then becoming available, including stone lintels, stained-glass windows, and gables.

Wellesley Ave.

402 Wellesley St.

The "Owl House," 402 Wellesley Street (26)

Named for the terracotta owl detail, this house was once home to illustrator Charles W. Jeffreys. It was built in 1893 by Jeffreys's father.

Alpha Avenue (27)

Another little street built entirely by only one builder, this in 1887 by William Bromely, who was also a plasterer. The local term "Alpha-style" used to describe

Alpha Ave.

working-class-sized Second Empire mansarded miniatures, such as those lining Geneva Street, were so called because of the style's use here.

Wellesley Cottages

Wellesley Cottages (28)

This private little lane not shown on city maps leads to a truly quaint row built in 1886. The award-winning design for these workers' cottages was featured at the London Exhibition of 1851. All have been completely modernized.

Laurier Avenue (29)

Like Wellesley Avenue, this entire street of 1889 Queen Anne Bay-n-Gables, as well as the two rows that flank it on Wellesley Street (316-324 and 326-334), are the work of builder Frank Armstrong.

Laurier Ave.

Continue west on Wellesley and turn north on Parliament.

St. James Cemetery

St. James Cemetery and St. James-the-Less Chapel (30)

This delightful 40-acre plot with its hills, winding walks, and glorious trees was laid out in 1845 by J.G. Howard to

568-582 Parliament St.

serve the burial needs of Toronto's elite. Family tombs bear the names Gooderham, Worts, Jarvis, Brock, Manning, and Howland among others. The chapel, constructed in 1858, was designed by architects Cumberland and Storm, and is widely considered one of the loveliest buildings in Canada.

Head back down Parliament to see a series of fine rows. Originally built as housing, some have been converted to commercial or mixed use, and one has become a hostel owned by the City of Toronto.

Chamberlin Terrace, 568-582 Parliament Street (31)

Builder Charles Chamberlin named this 1876 project, in this case an eight-unit Second Empire row, for himself.

Darling Terrace, 562-566 Parliament Street (32)

Not to be outdone, contractor William Darling named his highly Victorian triple, built the following year, for himself.

502-508 Parliament St.

502-508 Parliament Street (33)

Evidently more modest, builder J. Bowden, most of whose projects were east of the Don, chose to use only the street address when he built this grand Second Empire row of four in 1879.

Hotel Winchester, 531 Parliament Street (34)

Hotel Winchester

Hard though it may be to believe today, the Winchester, built in 1888 as the Lake View, was in its heyday considered a bucolic resort that boasted a good lawn, a beer garden, a belvedere atop its corner tower, an up-to-date fire alarm system, baths on every floor and, yes, a view of Lake Ontario.

562-566 Parliament St.

Rose Ave.

21 Winchester St.

The last section of the tour takes you through the portion of Cabbagetown west of Parliament and back towards Allan Gardens.

21 Winchester Street (35)
This 1863 Georgian home, an unusual style in Cabbagetown, was built as the rectory for nearby St. Peter's Church.

Rose Avenue (36)
The solid-looking six-unit row at 1-11 dates from 1879, except for number 5, which was demolished in the 1970s and later rebuilt. Thomas Bryce, a number of whose buildings were noted in the area east of Parliament, also built the doubles at 44-46 and 48-50 in 1887 and 1885 respectively.

Winchester Street Junior Public School (37)
By the time this 1898 massive-looking Queen Anne structure was completed — replacing a small 1874 school — it was already too small. Additions were made in 1901. Graduates include C.W. Jefferys and Walter Houston.

Winchester St. Junior Public School

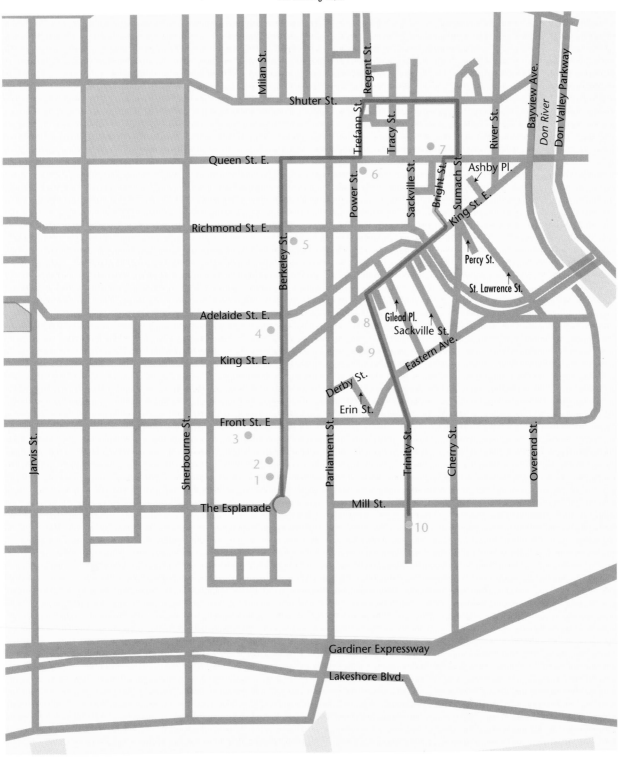

Tour Two: Cabbagetown's Roots

Courtyard, 2 Berkeley St.

Tour Two: Cabbagetown's Roots

Today's Cabbagetown has its roots in the area south of Dundas Street. In contrast to the "newer," northern part of the neighbourhood, it has been so altered over the years that many original sites can be difficult to find. This tour concentrates on four areas of interest: Berkeley Street from the Esplanade north to Queen Street, which was the western boundary of the Crown Lands that became Cabbagetown; Queen Street east of Berkeley, which was the Irish-Catholic centre of the old community; the cluster of homes and old shops near King and Trinity, which are adjacent to Little Trinity, its rectory, and Enoch Turner Schoolhouse; and the Gooderham and Worts site near Parliament and Mill Streets.

2 Berkeley Street (1)

The original 1797 Legislative Buildings for Upper Canada and the Berkeley Block House were located just a stone's throw from this collection of industrial buildings dating from the 1860s and 1870s. In the 1970s, they were combined into a single commercial building known as "Berkeley Castle" by owner, architect A. J. Diamond. The Castle boasts an interior courtyard, accessible from the Esplanade, that is arguably the most understated, sophisticated outdoor room in Toronto.

Canadian Stage Company, 24-26 Berkeley Street (2)

Many of the buildings in the immediate area were once part of the Consumers Gas Company's vast complex, and this, built between 1886 and 1892 and designed by Strickland & Symons, is one of them. In the 1970s, it was acquired by Canadian Stage.

Canadian Stage Company

Joey and Toby Tanenbaum Opera Centre, 239 and Canadian Opera Company, 223-237 Front Street (3)

Apart from performance space, all the Canadian Opera Company's operations are located here, in this collection of industrial buildings. The barn-like building at 239 was another Consumers Gas Company building, an 1887 purifying house. The remainder of the complex building

Joey and Toby Tanenbaum Opera Centre

was Standard Woolen Mills' 1882 factory, believed to have been designed by E.J. Lennox, architect of Toronto's Old City Hall. Completing the street front are the immediately adjacent buildings at 219-221 which date from 1885 and belonged to Leadley & Barber Woolen Mills and a cigar box manufacturer respectively.

Head north on Berkeley Street from here, past a variety of late nineteenth-century industrial and commercial buildings. The one on the southwest corner of King Street includes an unusual chamfered corner with a cast-iron column. Opposite, on the north side of King, stood Greenshields General Store built in 1845. At 55-77, there is an intact 1872 row of former homes, now small businesses, unusual for having been, in 1969, one of the first rehabilitation projects undertaken in the city.

Alumnae Theatre, 70 Berkeley Street (4)

A firehall was first built on this site in 1859. A flamboyant replacement was erected in 1903. The latter lost its tower in 1952 and was remodelled to serve as headquarters for Canada's oldest theatrical company, the University Alumnae Dramatic Club, in 1971.

Alumnae Theatre

115 Berkeley St.

St. Paul's Roman Catholic Church, 93 Power Street (6)

This grand 1887 Renaissance-style church, which boasts a remarkable, light-filled interior, was designed by architect Joseph Connolley to replace a far smaller 1826 church that served the working-class Catholic community clustered in this area. Ancillary to the church was the equally grand House of Providence (known by some wags as the House of Protestants) which was demolished to permit construction of ramps onto the Don Valley Parkway.

Sheldon Ward House, 115 Berkeley Street (5)

Ward was a brickmaker and city council member who died on a job site in 1846, a mere year after moving into his home, one of the oldest extant buildings in Toronto, albeit an extremely altered one.

A right turn at Queen Street takes you eastward toward the heart of today's "Corktown."

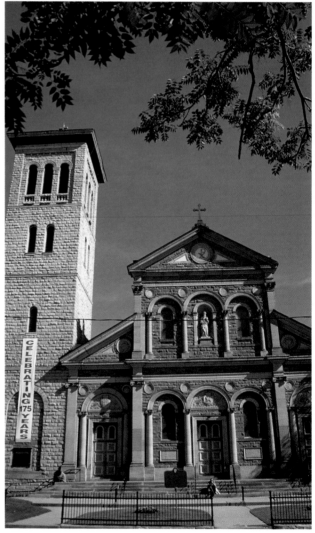

St. Paul's Roman Catholic Church

468-496 Queen St. E.

Dominion Brewery, 468-496 Queen Street East (7)

At least eight breweries were once scattered throughout Cabbagetown. It is fortunate that the only one remaining is the grandest. Built in the late 1870s by Robert Davies, scion of an old brewing family, the Don Brewery promoted Canadian ales and porters internationally. The striking red- and yellow-brick building has been completely renovated and is spurring redevelopment in the immediate neighbourhood.

Take a short jaunt northward from the Brewery, up Trefann, Tracy, or Sackville Streets to Shuter to get a look at the Trefann infill project. Just east of Tracy, at 383 Shuter, stands a unique landmark, a rather nondescript house only 2.5 metres wide — Toronto's

narrowest. A bit further east, at Sackville, is Park School, which boasts the grandest entrance of any of the city's elementary schools; it will be familiar to viewers of *Harriet the Spy* as the setting for numerous scenes.

Another short detour south of Queen Street en route to the next cluster of notable buildings will take you past the streets that look most like Cabbagetown in the old days, when it was entirely a working-class enclave. Bright Street, which cuts through from Queen to King Streets, is the most picturesque of these; tiny Ashby Place and Percy Streets, both just off King, are the most true to their original condition.

Now head back west along King.

Little Trinity Church

Little Trinity Church and Rectory, 425 and 417 King Street East (8)

The stories behind the construction of Little Trinity, and the Enoch Turner Schoolhouse just south of it, are told in Chapter 1. Suffice to say here that the working-class congregants who prevailed on their wealthier brethren to construct the church got a good deal. It is a delightful, unpretentious, well-proportioned Tudor Gothic miniature. Its 1853 rectory next door is nothing exciting, but its simplicity and contemporaneousness help make it a good partner for the church.

Enoch Turner Schoolhouse, 106 Trinity St. (9)

The province's first coeducational school is now a living museum, open at set hours and whenever the curator catches sight of anyone interested in the site. Its location behind Little Trinity creates a real sense of stepping back in time. The sensation is greatly enhanced by the presence of two rows of very well-preserved, unusually

Enoch Turner Schoolhouse

well-designed workers' cottages stretched along the length of Trinity Street opposite the institutional sites, and by the presence, on King Street, of two adjacent rows of similarly well-preserved commercial buildings.

Continue south on Trinity, all the way to Mill Street.

Gooderham and Worts Distillery, 55 Mill Street (10)

As described in Chapter 3, this 6-hectare site is now being refurbished and redeveloped to create a vibrant new neighbourhood. The most noteworthy buildings include David Roberts Sr.'s huge 1859 limestone grist mill and distillery — one of the few, and probably the largest limestone building ever built in Toronto — and the malt and storehouse additions by the well-known architectural firm of Gundry & Langley in 1863.

The Gooderham and Worts Distillery

INDEX